DIGITAL

ARMOR

The Confessions of a Reformed Hacker

Jacinto Luis Marques

EBOOK ISBN: 978-969-4692-07-4

PAPERBACK ISBN: 978-969-4692-08-1

HARDBACK ISBN: 978-969-4692-09-8

TABLE OF CONTENTS

PREFACE

This book thoroughly explores cybersecurity, providing valuable insights into the minds and tactics of hackers. Through clear explanations and relatable examples, readers gain a deeper understanding of the vulnerabilities present in digital systems. Individuals and organizations can enhance their defenses against cyberattacks by identifying common threats and vulnerabilities. Adequate security measures can be implemented with practical guidance on password management and personal information protection. The book places a strong emphasis on protecting mobile devices and home networks from social engineering attacks while encouraging vigilance. It provides readers with the information and resources needed to strengthen their cybersecurity posture and fend off new and emerging threats, with a focus on usability and practicality.

ABOUT THE AUTHOR

 Jacinto Marques is a seasoned cybersecurity advocate and architect, boasting extensive academic credentials, including a Bachelor's degree in Information Security, a Postgraduate degree in IT Governance, and a Master's degree in Cybersecurity from Webster University. With over 18 years of experience collaborating with government organizations, Marques has played a significant role in promoting defenses against cyber threats and ensuring the security of critical infrastructures. His unwavering dedication and innovative solutions have garnered him widespread recognition as a trusted advisor in the cybersecurity community.

With a wealth of experience and a robust educational background, Jacinto has achieved several prestigious certifications in the cybersecurity world. These include Certified Information Security Manager (CISM), Certified Ethical Hacker (CEH), The Open Group Architecture Framework (TOGAF), Threat Modeling Practitioner, AWS Certified Solutions Architect, AWS Certified Security – Specialty, CompTIA Security+, ISO 27001 Lead Implementer, ITIL Foundation, and Microsoft Certified Cybersecurity Expert.

ACKNOWLEDGEMENT

I extend my heartfelt gratitude to all those who played significant roles in creating and publishing "Digital Armor: Confession Of A Reformed Hacker." Your support, guidance, and encouragement were instrumental in bringing this book to fruition.

Special thanks go to my family for their unwavering love and support; to my friends and colleagues for their invaluable feedback and inspiration; to the dedicated publishing team for their professionalism; and to my readers and supporters for their engagement.

I am deeply grateful to Jesus Christ, my Lord, for His blessings and guidance. This book is a reflection of my experiences and is intended to inspire and educate its readers.

Jacinto Luis Marques

INTRODUCTION

A hacker is someone skilled in computer programming and network security who uses their expertise to access networks and computer systems without authorization. However, it's important to recognize that not all hackers have malicious intent. The hacker community is diverse, consisting of different groups with varying intentions and ethical standards.

One of the most common types of hackers is the "black hat" hacker. This group engages in illegal or malicious activities to exploit vulnerabilities for personal gain, such as stealing sensitive information, disrupting services, or deploying ransomware. These hackers often operate in secrecy, concealing their identities to evade detection and prosecution.

In contrast, "white hat" hackers, also known as ethical hackers or penetration testers, employ their skills for constructive purposes. They identify security weaknesses in systems and help organizations fortify their defenses. Working independently or with security firms, they assist clients in securing their networks and preventing cyber attacks.

Another category is "gray hat" hackers, who occupy the middle ground between black and white hat hackers. They may engage in technically illegal activities that are not inherently malicious, like breaching systems to expose vulnerabilities without causing harm.

While their actions may not always adhere to legal or ethical standards, they can sometimes be catalysts for improving cybersecurity by highlighting areas that require attention.

CHAPTER 1

Unveiling the Hacker's

Understanding The Motivations And Mindset Of Hackers

Understanding why hackers act the way they do is akin to unraveling the mysteries of human behavior. While many perceive hackers as troublemakers with malicious intentions, the reality is far more nuanced. Many hackers are primarily driven by a mindset of curiosity and exploration. Their fascination with technology stems from a genuine desire to understand how systems work and how they can be modified.

The hacker mindset is characterized by relentless problem-solving and creative thinking. Hackers see challenges not as barriers but as opportunities to extend the boundaries of the possible. They thrive in environments where ingenuity and innovation are paramount, constantly seeking new methods to circumvent security measures and discover vulnerabilities. This intrinsic drive to exceed limits distinguishes hackers from average users.

However, not all hackers share the same intentions. Some, known as white hat hackers, use their skills for positive purposes, while others might choose a darker path, exploiting vulnerabilities for personal gain or to create chaos. This dichotomy highlights the complexity of the hacker community and the varied motivations of its members.

There are risks associated with hacking, including significant legal and ethical implications that can lead to consequences such as fines, imprisonment, or reputational damage. Despite these dangers, many hackers are undeterred, believing the thrill of acquiring new information and the pursuit of knowledge outweigh potential risks.

Ultimately, the motivations and mindsets of hackers are as varied as the individuals themselves. While some are driven by altruism and the desire to improve the world, others are motivated by personal gain or a sense of rebellion.

Recognizing Common Vulnerabilities Exploited By Hackers

Hackers, armed with sophisticated tools and techniques, are constantly searching for vulnerabilities in our systems and networks to exploit for their gain. Understanding these vulnerabilities is crucial for safeguarding against potential attacks and protecting sensitive information.

A. Software Vulnerabilities:

Cyberattacks often stem from flaws in software systems. These vulnerabilities, ranging from simple coding errors to complex design flaws, provide hackers with opportunities to infiltrate and compromise systems. Common software vulnerabilities include buffer overflows, SQL injection, and cross-site scripting (XSS), each offering unique exploitation opportunities. Buffer overflows, resulting from writing data beyond a program's memory limits, can lead to unauthorized code execution. SQL injection attacks manipulate SQL queries to gain illegal access to databases, exploiting weaknesses in web application input validation. XSS attacks inject

13

malicious scripts into web pages, enabling attackers to steal sensitive information or hijack user sessions.

B. Phishing Attacks:

Phishing attacks, another prevalent tactic, exploit human vulnerabilities using psychological manipulation. These attacks often mimic official correspondence from trusted sources like banks or governments. Using social engineering techniques, hackers trick victims into clicking on malicious links, downloading malware-infested attachments, or disclosing personal information. The rise of spear phishing and whaling attacks, which tailor messages to specific individuals or organizations, highlights the evolving sophistication of phishing tactics.

C. Weak Authentication Mechanisms:

Weak or inadequate authentication practices present significant vulnerabilities. Hackers exploit common issues like default credentials, predictable passwords, and weak authentication protocols. They use techniques like brute force attacks, credential stuffing, and password spraying for unauthorized access. The widespread use of password-based authentication across platforms increases the risk of credential compromise. Organizations should adopt multifactor authentication (MFA) and implement strong password policies to enhance authentication security.

D. Misconfigurations:

Misconfigurations, often due to human error or complex IT environments, expose systems and networks to hacker exploitation.

Typical misconfigurations include improper access controls, unpatched software, and misaligned security policies. Hackers exploit these to gain unauthorized access to sensitive data or escalate privileges. Comprehensive configuration management and automated tools for detecting and remediating misconfigurations can reduce these vulnerabilities.

E. Insider Threats:

While external threats are often highlighted, insider threats are a significant risk. These include malicious actions by employees, contractors, or business partners. Motivations vary, from revenge-seeking employees to negligent or colluding insiders. Insider threats bypass traditional security controls, exploiting trust relationships. Monitoring user behavior, enforcing access controls, and fostering a security-aware culture can mitigate insider threat risks.

CHAPTER 2

The Anatomy of a Cyber Attack

Exploring Different Types of Cyber Threats

In today's digitally connected world, where transactions are completed with ease and information flows freely, the threat of cyberattacks has become more significant than ever. Understanding the structure of these attacks is crucial to prevent them and protect our digital lives.

Phishing is often regarded as one of the oldest tricks in the cybercriminal's playbook and remains a prevalent and effective method of attack. It involves deceiving unsuspecting individuals into revealing sensitive information such as passwords, credit card numbers, or personal data, by pretending to be a trustworthy entity. These deceptive emails, messages, or websites often convincingly mimic legitimate sources, making it hard for even discerning individuals to identify the deception. Cybercriminals use cunning social engineering strategies and psychological manipulation to exploit human weaknesses and gain unauthorized access to confidential data.

Malware, short for malicious software, represents another significant threat in cyberspace. Unlike phishing, which requires human interaction, malware operates autonomously, infecting systems and causing chaos without direct user intervention. Malware comes in various forms, from worms and viruses to trojans and spyware, with intentions ranging from disrupting operations to stealing sensitive data or turning compromised systems into botnets for further attacks. The increasing number of connected devices and the Internet of

Things (IoT) expands the potential attack surface for malware, posing a formidable challenge for defenders.

Ransomware, a particularly sinister cyber threat, holds organizations and individuals hostage by encrypting their data and demanding payment for its release. The evolution of ransomware from a niche concern to a global epidemic highlights its effectiveness and profitability for cybercriminals. Ransomware attacks can cause financial losses, operational disruptions, and compromised data integrity, commonly targeting vital infrastructure, healthcare facilities, and even entire cities. The emergence of ransomware-as-a-service (RaaS) models has made it simpler for aspiring cybercriminals to initiate complex attacks with minimal training.

Other cyber threats lurking in the digital shadows include Distributed Denial-of-Service (DDoS) attacks, which aim to render systems inoperable by overwhelming them with traffic. While DDoS attacks might not directly compromise data or systems, they cause significant damage by disrupting services and damaging reputations. Insider threats also pose a substantial challenge, as trusted individuals with privileged access might exploit their position to steal data, sabotage systems, or leak sensitive information.

Analyzing Real-Life Cyber Attack Scenarios And Their Consequences

A. Equifax Data Breach of 2017:

The Equifax data breach stands as a stark reminder of the devastating consequences of a significant cybersecurity failure. Hackers exploited a vulnerability in Equifax's web application, gaining unauthorized access to the personal information of over 147 million customers, including birthdates and Social Security numbers. The breach led to intense public scrutiny, regulatory investigations, and legal challenges for Equifax, eroding consumer trust and exposing systemic cybersecurity weaknesses. It highlighted the critical need for timely patch management, proactive vulnerability scanning, and effective incident response protocols.

B. WannaCry Ransomware Outbreak of 2017:

The WannaCry ransomware outbreak demonstrated the catastrophic impact of unpatched vulnerabilities and malware's rapid spread across networks. Exploiting a leaked NSA exploit, WannaCry targeted outdated Microsoft Windows versions, infecting and encrypting hundreds of thousands of computers globally. The attack underscored the importance of regular software updates, patching, and backup and recovery mechanisms. It also highlighted the need for global collaboration and proactive, multi-layered cybersecurity approaches.

C. SolarWinds Supply Chain Compromise of 2020:

The SolarWinds incident marked a new era in cyber surveillance, showcasing sophisticated, nation-state-sponsored attacks on critical infrastructure and government agencies. Attackers infiltrated SolarWinds' software supply chain, embedding malicious code into seemingly legitimate updates. This breach underscored the importance of enhanced supply chain security, rigorous vendor risk management, and continuous monitoring and threat detection. It also emphasized the challenges in cyber attack attribution and response.

D. Colonial Pipeline Ransomware Attack (2021):

The 2021 ransomware attack on Colonial Pipeline, operating the largest fuel pipeline in the U.S., had significant and far-reaching effects. This attack, executed by the DarkSide cybergang, disrupted fuel supplies on the East Coast, leading to panic buying and price hikes. The incident underlined the vulnerabilities of critical infrastructure to cyber attacks, economic impacts on dependent industries, and the necessity for robust cyber resilience and incident response strategies.

E. Microsoft Exchange Server Breach (2023):

In 2023, state-sponsored threat actors exploited vulnerabilities in Microsoft Exchange Server, known collectively as ProxyLogon, leading to unauthorized data access and disruptions in affected networks. The breach had significant repercussions, including data breaches and operational disruptions, and emphasized the importance of timely patch management, enhanced threat intelligence sharing, and the development of effective cybersecurity strategies.

CHAPTER 3

Strengthening Your Digital Fortress

The Fundamentals Of Cybersecurity Hygiene

Cyber threats come in various forms, from government attacks to actions by individuals seeking monetary gain. Understanding the motives and methods behind these threats is key to building robust defenses and maintaining online safety.

A. Embracing a Multi-Layered Approach:

Firewalls serve as our first line of defense, controlling traffic flow and blocking unauthorized access. Beyond this, we deploy intrusion detection systems, constantly scanning for suspicious activity. Antivirus software further strengthens our defenses, ready to combat viruses, malware, and other online threats. Integrating these layers forms a comprehensive strategy that minimizes successful cyber attacks and protects our digital assets.

B. Practicing Good Cyber Hygiene:

Regularly updating operating systems and software is essential to close off vulnerabilities. Strong, unique passwords for internet accounts are crucial for security. Enabling two-factor authentication adds an additional layer of defense. Being cautious with links or attachments from unknown sources is vital to avoid phishing and malware. Implementing strong user permissions and access controls in organizations prevents unauthorized access to sensitive information.

C. Educating and Empowering Users:

Customized training programs for employees are crucial. These should include education on social engineering techniques, phishing awareness, and best practices for handling sensitive information. Fostering a culture of cybersecurity awareness and accountability within organizations is also important, as is encouraging proactive cybersecurity behaviors.

D. Securing the Supply Chain:

Vetting third-party vendors thoroughly is essential for supply chain security. Contractual obligations for security compliance must be established. Proactive monitoring for malicious activities or supply chain intrusions is crucial. Maintaining customer trust and loyalty is equally important, and this is achieved by demonstrating commitment to supply chain security.

E. Investing in Emerging Technologies:

AI and machine learning are game-changers in combating cyber threats, providing tools for data analysis, pattern recognition, and anomaly detection. Blockchain technology offers secure data storage and transfer solutions, while secure hardware solutions are key to protecting against physical attacks and unauthorized access. Investment in research and development, as well as collaboration with industry partners and academic institutions, is critical for innovation in cybersecurity.

F. Fostering Collaboration and Information Sharing:

Cybersecurity requires collective effort and collaboration across sectors and stakeholders. Sharing threat intelligence and best practices is vital to improve detection, response, and recovery from cyber attacks. By fostering a culture of collaboration and information sharing, we can enhance the collective defense against cyber threats and strengthen the digital ecosystem's resilience.

Best Practices for Password Management and Authentication

A. Creating Strong and Unique Passwords:

A strong password is more than just a random sequence of characters; it's a vital shield against relentless cyber threats. Creating strong and unique passwords involves:

1. Complexity and Length:

A robust password typically includes a mix of uppercase and lowercase letters, numbers, and symbols. Aim for a length of at least 12 to 16 characters, as longer passwords are generally more secure.

2. Unpredictability:

Avoid common phrases, easily guessable information (like birthdates or names), and repetitive or sequential characters. The key is to be unpredictable and avoid patterns that are easy for attackers to guess.

3. Originality:

Each account should have its unique password. Reusing passwords across multiple platforms increases the risk that a breach on one site could compromise your security elsewhere.

4. Password Managers:

Consider using a password manager to generate and store complex passwords. These tools can create highly secure passwords and keep them safe, alleviating the burden of having to remember each one.

5. Regular Updates:

Change your passwords regularly, especially if you suspect a breach. Frequent updates can help prevent unauthorized access and maintain account security.

By adhering to these principles, you create a formidable barrier against unauthorized access, safeguarding your digital identity and sensitive information from potential cyber threats.

In the midst of a relentless onslaught of cyber threats seeking to breach our defenses, creating strong and unique passwords is more than a mere security measure. It is a testament to our dedication to safeguarding our digital identities and preserving the integrity of our online domains. This proactive approach is crucial in combating the wave of cyberattacks that threaten our sense of privacy and security in the digital realm.

Strong, distinctive passwords are our bulwark against the forces that seek to undermine our online security. They are not just barriers; they are expressions of our commitment to maintaining control over our digital lives. In an era where our personal and professional lives are increasingly conducted online, robust password practices are fundamental to ensuring that our virtual presence remains secure and inviolate.

By adopting this mindset, we do more than just protect individual accounts; we contribute to the broader effort of fortifying the digital landscape against the ever-evolving threats that lurk within it. Our unique passwords are not just keys to our online profiles; they are shields wielded in the ongoing battle for digital security and privacy.

Your focus on the critical elements of strong password creation is well-articulated. Here's a refined version for enhanced clarity and emphasis:

The essence of a strong password lies in its complexity. Creating a robust password involves much more than selecting a meaningful word or phrase. It requires a mix of uppercase and lowercase letters, numbers, and special characters, forming an impenetrable barrier against unauthorized access. By weaving together a diverse array of characters, we establish layers of complexity that confound even the most skilled cybercriminals.

Furthermore, the significance of uniqueness in password creation cannot be overlooked. Just as we wouldn't use a single key for every lock in our physical world, employing unique passwords for each online account is essential to protect our digital realms. This practice shields our accounts from the cascading effects of a single security breach. Diversifying our passwords across different accounts effectively minimizes the risk of multiple accounts being compromised by a single password breach.

In an era where our digital identities are increasingly intertwined with our daily lives, strong and distinctive passwords are crucial. They empower us, giving us control over our online security and serving as the first line of defense against cyber threats. By committing to the creation of strong passwords, we not only safeguard our personal information but also contribute to the collective security and resilience of the online community.

6. Regularly Updating Passwords:

Changing passwords regularly is more than just a good habit; it's a proactive measure essential in times of uncertainty. This practice strengthens our online identities and fortifies our digital defenses against the unceasing onslaught of cyberattacks.

The principle behind frequent password changes is to always remain one step ahead of potential adversaries. By routinely updating our passwords, we maintain a decisive edge in the ever-changing landscape of cyber threats. This habit disrupts the patterns that hackers might exploit, significantly reducing their chances of gaining unauthorized access. Regular password changes, whether every few months or immediately following a suspected security breach, are key in minimizing vulnerabilities.

Moreover, the practice of frequently changing passwords underscores the dynamic nature of cybersecurity. In a digital world where threats rapidly evolve and adversaries constantly devise new strategies, complacency is not viable. We must be agile, continually adapting and evolving to match the pace of the ever-shifting cyber threat environment. Regular password updates are a critical part of this process, reinforcing our digital fortresses and addressing potential weaknesses before they can be exploited.

A. Leveraging Password Managers

Password managers are not merely tools; they symbolize trust and reliability. Their ability to generate, store, and autofill complex passwords for numerous online accounts positions them as beacons of security in the precarious digital world. The true value of password managers lies in transcending human memory limitations. They serve as dependable allies in our digital journey, easing the burden of remembering myriad login credentials, thereby empowering us with confidence.

These managers do more than store passwords; they fortify our virtual strongholds against relentless cyberattacks. Offering a secure and streamlined solution to password management, they enable us to reclaim control of our digital spaces, asserting our presence in the digital realm.

Utilizing password managers is a practical approach to handling the complexities of password management. It also signifies our commitment to securing our digital assets and identities. By entrusting our passwords to these vigilant guardians, we pave the way for a safer digital future, where our online sanctuaries stand shielded from the lurking threats of the digital world.

B. Implementing Multifactor Authentication (MFA)

MFA exemplifies resilience through diversity. Combining a password with a mobile device or security token, MFA erects a formidable barrier that thwarts even the most persistent adversaries. This method transcends traditional password-only authentication, countering its vulnerabilities in an era where password breaches are all too common. By incorporating additional authentication factors like biometric data or one-time passcodes, MFA ensures our digital realms are tightly guarded against unauthorized entry.

C. Educating Users About Password Hygiene

Dedicated training programs on password hygiene are more than instructional guides; they light the way to digital resilience. These programs empower users with the knowledge of crafting secure passwords and understanding the logic behind each safety measure.

Educated users can adeptly avoid common pitfalls like predictable passwords, repeated credentials, or insecure storage, becoming architects of their digital safety.

Such education transforms users from passive receivers of information into active participants in the battle for digital security. They embody empowerment, navigating their digital lives with deliberate password choices, vigilant online behavior, and informed responses. In doing so, they reshape the narrative of cybersecurity from a complex challenge into a journey of self-awareness and resilience.

CHAPTER 4

Safeguarding Your Online Identity

Protecting Personal Information From Data Breaches

Email addresses and credit card numbers are just a few examples of the data that constitute our digital identities, each with its own importance. Acknowledging the potential consequences of a data breach, from financial loss to identity theft, is crucial for maintaining vigilance in protecting this information.

Strong, Unique Passwords:

Using strong, unique passwords is a fundamental practice for securing our accounts. A password acts as the initial barrier against unauthorized access. Complex passwords that combine letters, numbers, and symbols enhance security. Moreover, different passwords for each account reduce the risk of widespread compromise in a breach.

Two-Factor Authentication (2FA):

2FA provides an additional layer of security. It typically combines something you know (a password) with something you have (e.g., a code sent to your phone), significantly mitigating the risk of password theft.

Staying Informed:

Remaining updated on security threats and vulnerabilities is vital. Subscribing to reliable security publications and following reputable cybersecurity blogs offers insights into cybercrime trends, software vulnerabilities, and emerging attack methods. This information helps individuals anticipate and prevent potential threats to their digital assets.

Careful Information Sharing Online:

Each piece of personal information shared online, whether on social media, e-commerce sites, or through posts and comments, is a fragment of your digital identity exposed. Practicing discernment in what and where you share is critical. Understanding and adjusting privacy settings on various platforms can help limit unnecessary data exposure.

Safe Browsing Habits:

Practicing safe browsing habits, such as verifying website legitimacy, avoiding suspicious links, and using reputable antivirus software, reduces the risk of phishing and malware. Regular backups to external drives or cloud storage safeguard essential data against loss, while employing VPNs when using public Wi-Fi adds an additional security layer.

Device Security:

Keeping devices updated with the latest security patches and being cautious with public Wi-Fi connections are essential steps in protecting against unauthorized access. Utilizing VPN services when connecting to public networks further encrypts and protects your internet traffic.

By implementing these practices, individuals can significantly enhance their online security, minimizing the risk of data breaches and protecting their digital identities.

Managing online accounts and privacy settings effectively

Facebook

Privacy Settings: Think of your Facebook profile as your digital sanctuary. Regularly reviewing and adjusting your privacy settings is essential. These settings control who can view your posts, photos, and personal information. By taking charge of your privacy settings, you empower yourself to safeguard your online privacy, ensuring that you share content confidently and securely. This proactive approach helps manage your digital footprint and maintain control over your personal data on social media.

Friend Requests: Be vigilant when it comes to accepting friend requests. It's important to connect only with individuals you know and trust. Cultivating genuine relationships based on understanding and respect is key. Prioritize quality over quantity in your online connections to ensure a meaningful and secure network. This approach not only enhances your online experience but also serves as a safeguard against potential privacy breaches and cyber threats that can arise from indiscriminate online connections.

Your focus on online privacy and security for Facebook and Twitter is essential. Here's a revised version for clarity and conciseness:

Facebook: Avoid Oversharing

1. Sensitive: Information: Refrain from publicly sharing personal details on your profile to protect your privacy.

2. Vigilance: Be aware of the potential risks and vulnerabilities associated with sharing information online.

3. Discretion: Shape a digital footprint that truly represents your best self by sharing mindfully.

By valuing privacy, selective connections, and thoughtful sharing, you can confidently and authentically engage on Facebook.

Twitter: Secure Your Account

1. Account Privacy: Consider setting your Twitter account to private. This lets you control who sees your tweets and manages your follower requests, creating a safer space for expression.

2. Secure Passwords: Use strong, unique passwords for your Twitter account and enable two-factor authentication. This step is vital for protecting your digital identity.

3.Phishing Awareness: Be wary of direct messages with links or attachments, as they might be phishing attempts. Staying alert helps safeguard your account from unauthorized access or malicious activities.

Instagram:

1. Private Account: Setting your account to private gives you control over who sees your content, fostering a safer and more intimate sharing environment.

2. Geotagging: Turn off geotagging to keep your location private and enhance your online safety.

3.Report: Suspicious Activity: Reporting any abusive behavior helps maintain a safe and inclusive platform for all users.

LinkedIn:

1. Profile Privacy: Customize your profile settings to control who sees your professional information.

2. Network Wisely: Connect with trusted professional contacts to build a meaningful network.

3. Secure Communications: Use LinkedIn's messaging system for professional interactions, keeping personal contact information private.

WhatsApp:

1. End-to-End Encryption: Utilize this feature for secure, private communication.

2. Beware of Scams: Stay vigilant against phishing attempts and fraudulent messages.

3.Verify Contacts: Confirm the identity of contacts before sharing sensitive information.

Snapchat:

1. Privacy Settings: Adjust your settings to control who sees your content.

2. Limit Location Sharing: Disable location sharing to maintain privacy.

3.Be Selective with Friends: Add only known and trusted individuals.

YouTube:

1.Privacy Settings: Manage who can view and interact with your content.

2.Secure Account: Use strong passwords and enable two-factor authentication.

3.Avoid Clickbait:: Stay cautious of misleading titles and thumbnails.

Gmail:

1.Secure Passwords: Use a strong, unique password for your account.

2.Beware of Phishing: Be alert to suspicious emails and links.

3.Review Account Activity: Regularly monitor your account for unauthorized access.

Reddit:

1. Account Security: Protect your Reddit account with a robust password.

2. Community Engagement: Share cautiously and respect community guidelines.

3. Report Abuse: Act against any abusive behavior to maintain a positive environment.

Online Shopping Platforms:

1. Shop from Trusted Sellers: Choose reputable sellers with positive feedback.

2. Secure Payment Methods: Use safe payment options like credit cards or PayPal.

Mobile Banking Apps:

1. Secure Passwords and Biometric Authentication: Enhance security with strong passwords and biometric features.

2. Keep App Updated: Regularly update the app for the latest security patches.

3. Secure Network: Use secure networks, avoiding public Wi-Fi for transactions.

4. Beware of Phishing: Stay cautious of suspicious messages and calls.

5. Verify Transactions: Regularly check transaction history for unauthorized activities.

6. Logout After Use: Always log out after completing transactions.

7. Enable Account Alerts: Set up alerts for unusual account activities.

8. Report Lost or Stolen Devices: Immediately report any loss or theft of your device to your bank.

CHAPTER 5

Defending Against Social Engineering Techniques

Recognizing And Avoiding Social Engineering Attacks

Social engineering attacks, distinct from traditional cyber threats, exploit human psychology and behavior. These attacks manipulate trust, empathy, and cognitive biases to trick people into revealing private information or acting against their interests. Recognizing these attacks involves understanding the interplay between human interaction and manipulation.

At the heart of social engineering is psychological manipulation. Cybercriminals use this technique to exploit human traits, bypassing technical defenses by tapping into vulnerabilities inherent in human nature. These attacks rely more on deception and manipulation than on technical prowess, using persuasion to exploit the trust we place in familiar entities.

Social engineers often create elaborate narratives or assume false identities to invoke urgency or empathy, clouding judgment and masquerading as legitimate requests. This approach blurs the lines between reality and deception, leading individuals to unknowingly compromise their own security.

Key tactics in social engineering include:

1. Phishing: This involves impersonating trusted entities through fraudulent emails or messages, luring recipients into disclosing sensitive information or clicking on harmful links.

2. Pretexting: Here, attackers fabricate scenarios, manipulating individuals to divulge information under false pretenses.

By understanding these tactics and maintaining a healthy skepticism, individuals can better protect themselves against such sophisticated attacks, safeguarding their information and maintaining the integrity of their online interactions.

Recognizing and Avoiding Social Engineering Attacks

Social engineering attacks exploit human trust and empathy, often manipulating victims into compromising their security. Recognizing these attacks requires understanding psychological tactics used by cybercriminals.

1. Understanding Phishing: This technique exploits trust in authority or familiar institutions, manipulating emotions to elicit sensitive information or prompt action on malicious links. Cybercriminals may impersonate reputable organizations or create urgent situations to trigger immediate responses.

2. Identifying Pretexting: This method involves crafting false narratives or emergencies to deceive targets into divulging information. Success depends on the attacker's ability to evoke empathy, urgency, or fear through convincing stories.

Awareness and skepticism are key defenses against these tactics. Understanding psychological principles and familiarizing oneself with common social engineering strategies can help in identifying potential threats.

3. Maintaining Awareness: Staying informed about the latest cybersecurity trends and recognizing social engineering signs, such as phishing and pretexting, is vital. This involves learning about various tactics and their indicators.

4. Exercising Skepticism: Adopting a cautious approach when dealing with digital communications is crucial. This includes scrutinizing unexpected requests and verifying the legitimacy of communications through trusted channels.

5. Implementing Strong Security Measures: Setting precise procedures for handling confidential data and confirming identities is essential. Encouraging a culture of vigilance within organizations through training and awareness campaigns is equally important.

6. Utilizing Multi-Factor Authentication: This is an effective measure against social engineering, requiring multiple forms of verification to access sensitive information.

By combining these approaches, individuals and organizations can significantly bolster their defenses against the subtle yet potent threat of social engineering.

Strengthening Security Measures Against Social Engineering

In response to the threat of social engineering attacks, it's crucial to implement layered security strategies:

1. Multi-Factor Authentication: Adding multiple verification layers on top of traditional password authentication significantly reduces the risk of unauthorized access and the impact of credential theft and phishing scams.

2. Encryption: Encrypting data in transit and at rest is critical for protecting sensitive information from illegal access or interception. This method maintains data confidentiality and integrity, even during breaches.

3. Access Controls: Implementing granular access restrictions based on the least privilege principle helps minimize the risk of insider threats and unauthorized access. Limiting access to sensitive information ensures that only authorized users can reach critical data.

Remaining Vigilant and Adaptive

In the ever-evolving landscape of cybersecurity, vigilance and adaptability are key:

Vigilance: Staying informed about the latest threats, trends, and tactics used by cybercriminals helps in recognizing signs of social engineering. Awareness of the changing cybersecurity environment allows for proactive risk identification and mitigation.

Adaptability: Continuously adjusting and improving security practices is essential to combat new challenges and vulnerabilities. This involves implementing additional security layers, enhancing training, or using advanced technologies for real-time attack detection.

Being proactive is critical in this approach. Anticipating potential threats and adjusting tactics accordingly helps stay one step ahead of cybercriminals. Proactive defense strategies, rather than reactive ones, are essential in the fight against social engineering attacks.

Defending Against Social Engineering Techniques and Cybersecurity

A. Self-awareness and introspection

Self-awareness and introspection are foundational in

Key Skills for Defending Against Social Engineering in Cybersecurity

- Recognizing personal vulnerabilities, fears, and insecurities that attackers might exploit.

- Understanding and mitigating biases and preconceived notions that can be manipulated.

- Developing defense mechanisms through introspection to resist social engineering.

B. Emotional Intelligence

- Identifying and controlling emotions to reduce vulnerability to manipulation.

- Recognizing emotional triggers in social engineering attacks, like phishing or deceptive calls.

- Managing emotions in high-pressure situations to make rational decisions.

- Utilizing empathy to understand attacker motivations and protect oneself and others.

C. Critical Thinking

- Assessing information critically to identify manipulation or deception.

- Questioning the authenticity of messages and verifying sources.

- Challenging personal beliefs about security to identify vulnerabilities.

- Developing a habit of skepticism and independent thinking.

D. Establishing Healthy Boundaries

- Setting clear limits on shared information and access levels.

- Using assertive communication to enforce boundaries and express preferences.

- Recognizing and responding to boundary violations to deter attackers.

- Implementing consequences for violations to reinforce personal security.

E. Interpersonal Skills

- Communicating effectively to convey concerns and collaborate against attacks.

- Building empathy to understand and anticipate attacker strategies.

- Using conflict resolution skills to address disputes constructively and prevent divisions.

CHAPTER 6

Securing Your Home Network

Understanding The Vulnerabilities of Home Networks

Vulnerabilities in Home Networks and Cybersecurity Measures

1. Complexity of Connected Devices: The diverse range of smart devices in homes increases the attack surface, providing multiple entry points for hackers. Each connected device, from smart TVs to voice assistants, is a potential vulnerability.

2. Difficulty in Managing Network Security: The intricacy of managing multiple devices with varying configurations makes it hard to maintain comprehensive network security. This can lead to oversight and unaddressed vulnerabilities.

3. Software Updates: Often, users neglect to regularly update the firmware and software of routers, modems, and devices, leaving exploitable gaps. Cybercriminals target these outdated systems to gain unauthorized network access.

4. Router Updates: Failing to update router firmware is a common security gap. Regular updates are essential to close vulnerabilities that could be exploited by attackers.

5. Weak or Default Passwords: Using weak or default passwords is a significant risk. Cybercriminals use these as easy entry points to infiltrate home networks and access sensitive data.

6. Consequences of Security Neglect: Neglecting network security can lead to severe outcomes like financial loss, reputation damage, and privacy breaches. Unauthorized network access can compromise personal and financial information.

Preventative Measures:

- Regularly update all connected devices and router firmware to patch vulnerabilities.

- Use strong, unique passwords and change default passwords on all devices.

- Enable automatic updates where possible to ensure timely security patches.

- Be vigilant and proactive in managing and securing home network components.

Cybersecurity Risks in Home Wi-Fi Networks and the Importance of Network Segmentation

1. Good Password Hygiene: Regularly updating and not reusing passwords across multiple accounts are crucial steps to secure home networks. Changing passwords periodically helps prevent unauthorized access.

2. Risks of Unencrypted Wi-Fi: Lack of proper encryption, like WPA2 or WPA3, makes networks susceptible to cybercriminal activities. Unencrypted data can be easily intercepted, leading to identity theft and financial fraud.

3. Man-in-the-Middle Attacks: Insecure networks allow attackers to intercept communications, tricking users into revealing sensitive information or installing malware.

4. Network Interconnectivity Risks: In a network where all devices are interconnected without segmentation, a breach in one device can compromise the entire network. This interconnectedness can result in significant financial and reputational damage.

5. Importance of Network Segmentation: Segmenting a network into separate subnetworks or VLANs can contain breaches and restrict lateral movement of attackers. This isolation is crucial in minimizing the impact of a cyberattack and protecting sensitive data.

By implementing network segmentation and maintaining robust encryption protocols, users can significantly enhance the security of their home Wi-Fi networks, safeguarding against a range of cyber threats.

Implementing Robust Security Measures For Routers And Connected Devices

Strategies for Enhancing Home Network Security

1. Regular Firmware Updates: Keep routers and connected devices updated with the latest firmware and security patches from manufacturers. This is essential for addressing vulnerabilities that could be exploited by cybercriminals.

2. Strong Passwords and Authentication: Replace default passwords with strong, unique passwords. Where possible, implement multi-factor authentication to prevent unauthorized access.

3. Encryption Protocols: Use encryption methods like WPA2 or WPA3 for wireless communications. This secures data transmission against eavesdropping and interception.

4. Disabling Unnecessary Features: Turn off features that are not in use, such as remote management, UPnP, and WPS, to reduce the network's attack surface.

5. Network Segmentation and Isolation: Segmenting the network into different areas for IoT devices, personal computers, and guest access can limit the impact of attacks and restrict lateral movement of potential threats.

6. Monitoring and Intrusion Detection: Implement intrusion detection and prevention systems (IDPS) to monitor network traffic for suspicious activities. Regularly log and analyze network activity for insights into potential security incidents.

7. Incident Response Planning: Develop a robust plan for responding to security breaches. This should include protocols for incident detection, containment, eradication, and recovery to minimize impact and facilitate a swift response.

CHAPTER 7

Navigating the World of Mobile Security

Mobile Threats and Vulnerabilities: Navigating the Risks

1. Malware Threats: Malware, a significant risk in the mobile ecosystem, includes various malicious programs like trojans and ransomware. It can infiltrate devices through malicious apps, compromised websites, and phishing attacks, posing severe risks like identity theft and financial loss.

2. Consequences of Malware: Once malware gains access to a device, it can collect private information, monitor user activity, and control key device functions, leading to significant privacy and security breaches.

3.Preventive Measures:

- Antivirus Software: Installing reputable antivirus software for mobile devices is crucial. These solutions detect and neutralize threats before they cause damage.

- Regular Updates: Keeping device firmware and apps updated is vital. Updates often include security patches addressing vulnerabilities that malware exploits.

- Download Caution: Exercise caution when downloading apps or clicking links. Verify app permissions, read reviews, and avoid suspicious links in emails or messages.

4. Combating Malware: A multi-faceted approach combining technological defenses and user awareness is essential. Staying informed about threats and practicing vigilance can significantly enhance mobile security.

In summary, mindfulness and proactive security measures are paramount in protecting against malware and maintaining digital wellbeing in the mobile landscape.

Phishing Attacks

Understanding Phishing Attacks in Mobile Security

Phishing attacks pose a significant threat to mobile users through their deceptive and sophisticated nature.

These attacks involve cybercriminals cunningly masquerading as trustworthy entities to dupe users into revealing sensitive information. The goal is often to obtain login credentials, financial details, or other personal data.

1. Deceptive Techniques: Phishing often employs emails, text messages, or app notifications that appear legitimate but are, in fact, fraudulent. The attackers meticulously craft these communications to mimic the style and language of reputable organizations, such as banks, government agencies, or popular online services.

2. Targets of Phishing: The primary target of phishing is the user's private and sensitive information. By convincing users to enter their details into fake websites or reply to fraudulent messages, attackers can gain unauthorized access to accounts, financial resources, and personal data.

3. Consequences of Phishing: Falling victim to a phishing attack can lead to severe repercussions, including financial loss, identity theft, and unauthorized access to personal and professional accounts.

Awareness and caution are key in protecting against phishing attacks in the mobile domain. Users should be skeptical of unsolicited messages, verify the authenticity of requests for personal information, and avoid clicking on links or downloading attachments from unknown or suspicious sources.

Key Mobile Security Threats and Mitigation Strategies

1. Malware Protection: Regularly update device firmware and applications to guard against malware. Install reputable antivirus software and be cautious with app downloads and email links.

2. Phishing Vigilance: Cultivate skepticism towards unsolicited communications and verify sender identities through trusted channels. Be cautious when sharing sensitive information.

3. Data Breaches: Implement robust security measures like encryption for stored data and secure communication channels. Use encrypted messaging apps, VPNs, and ensure strong password protection.

4. Network Spoofing: Avoid unsecured Wi-Fi networks and verify network authenticity before connecting. Employ VPNs for secure data transmission and disable automatic network connections on devices.

5. Unauthorized Cloud Access: Use multi-factor authentication, strong passwords, and routinely check access logs. Be alert to phishing attempts and use encrypted communication methods.

6. Man-in-the-Middle (MitM) Attacks: Employ encrypted communication protocols like HTTPS and SSL/TLS. Be cautious when using public Wi-Fi networks and utilize VPNs for added security.

7. SIM Swapping: Secure physical access to SIM cards, use alternative two-factor authentication methods, and be vigilant about unusual account activities. Regularly monitor account access and report any suspicious activity.

8. Advanced Persistent Threats (APTs): Adopt a multi-layered security approach with user vigilance, Mobile Device Management (MDM) programs, and network intrusion detection systems. Stay informed with threat intelligence feeds and practice regular incident response drills.

CHAPTER 8

The Role of Encryption and VPNs

Understanding Encryption And Its Importance

The Importance of Encryption in the Digital Age

1. Privacy Protection: Encryption is a key defender of privacy in the digital world. It secures personal communications like emails and messages, protecting them from unauthorized surveillance and data collection. This empowers individuals to maintain control over their personal information.

2. Security Enhancement: Essential for safeguarding data against cyber threats, encryption protects data both at rest and in transit. It deters cybercriminals, preserves the integrity of digital transactions, and enhances the security of sensitive information.

3. Compliance and Regulation: Encryption is critical for meeting data protection laws and industry-specific regulations. It helps organizations avoid legal consequences and reputational damage by ensuring compliance and demonstrating commitment to data privacy.

4. Intellectual Property Protection: In safeguarding intellectual property, encryption is invaluable. It secures proprietary data and research, preventing unauthorized access and maintaining a competitive edge while facilitating secure collaboration.

5. Freedom of Expression: Encryption is crucial for upholding freedom of expression, especially in restrictive environments. It enables secure communication for activists, journalists, and others, protecting them from censorship and surveillance.

6. Trust and Transparency: Encryption builds trust and transparency in digital interactions. It assures stakeholders of data security and enhances the credibility of digital platforms, from e-commerce to messaging.

Encryption Algorithms

Understanding Symmetric and Asymmetric Encryption, and the Role of VPNs

1. Symmetric Encryption: Characterized by its simplicity and efficiency, symmetric encryption uses a single key for both encryption and decryption. Ideal for encrypting large volumes of data quickly, it highlights the power of simplicity in cybersecurity solutions.

2. Asymmetric Encryption: This encryption method operates with two keys – one for encryption and another for decryption, ensuring secure communication and digital authentication. Asymmetric encryption is fundamental in facilitating secure online transactions and digital signatures, emphasizing collaboration and trust.

3. The Importance of VPNs:

Enhanced Privacy and Security: VPNs create a private, encrypted tunnel for internet data, protecting online activities from external surveillance and cyber threats.

- Anonymity and Access: Using a VPN masks your IP address and location, allowing access to geo-restricted content and preserving online anonymity.

- Safeguarding Sensitive Data: Particularly crucial for corporate networks, VPNs ensure secure remote connections, protecting sensitive business communications and data privacy in the era of remote work.

Each of these technologies plays a vital role in safeguarding digital integrity and confidentiality, reflecting the importance of robust cybersecurity practices in today's interconnected world.

CHAPTER 9

Securing Your Network.

Understanding Common Types of VPNs and How to Use Them

1. Remote Access VPNs: Ideal for individual users needing to access a private network remotely, like employees working from home. Requires VPN client software to connect to a server managed by the organization.

2. Site-to-Site VPNs: Used by organizations to connect multiple networks, such as branch offices. Configured with VPN routers or firewalls at each location, they enable secure communication across networks.

3. SSL/TLS VPNs: Provide secure remote access to web-based applications through standard web browsers. Suitable for accessing intranets, email servers, or web resources without special client software.

4. IPsec VPNs: Secure IP network transmissions, commonly used in enterprise environments for site-to-site and remote access VPNs. Implemented in tunnel or transport modes to encrypt and authenticate data.

5. OpenVPN: An open-source, highly customizable protocol that supports various encryption and authentication methods. Offers flexibility and cross-platform compatibility.

Using a VPN Effectively:

A. Select a Reliable VPN Provider: Focus on strong encryption, privacy policies, server options, and user-friendly applications.

B. Install VPN Client Software: Download and configure the VPN client on your device, adhering to the provider's installation guide.

C. Connect to a VPN Server: Log in and select a server location. Closer servers typically offer faster speeds, while distant servers can bypass regional content restrictions.

D. Secure Your Connection: Establish the VPN tunnel and activate additional features like split tunneling or a kill switch for enhanced security.

E. Verify Your Connection: Check your VPN's effectiveness by verifying IP addresses and conducting leak tests to ensure data encryption and routing are working correctly.

F. Browse Securely: With the VPN connection active, use the internet with the assurance that your data and privacy are protected through encryption.

CHAPTER 10

Protecting Your Digital Assets

Securing Financial Data and Online Transactions

1. Implement Robust Security Measures: Regular software updates and reliable antivirus protection are vital. Proactive security measures minimize the risk of unauthorized access and malware attacks.

2. Promote Awareness and Education: Understanding common cyber threats, such as phishing and fraudulent websites, is crucial. Educate about cyber hygiene practices, including the use of strong passwords and avoiding public Wi-Fi for financial transactions.

3. Ensure Secure Connections: Use HTTPS websites for financial transactions. Encrypted connections prevent data interception by cybercriminals.

4.Use Trusted Platforms: Conduct transactions through reputable financial institutions and online merchants with robust security protocols to reduce the risk of fraud.

5. Regular Account Monitoring: Frequently review bank and credit card statements for unauthorized activities and report suspicious transactions promptly.

6. Effective Password Management: Use strong, unique passwords for each online account. Password managers can assist in generating and storing secure passwords.

7. Limit Personal Information Sharing: Be cautious with the amount of personal information shared online to prevent identity theft and fraud.

8. Use Secure Wi-Fi Networks: Avoid public Wi-Fi for sensitive transactions. Use encrypted, password-protected networks for enhanced security.

9. Verify Two-way Communication: Confirm the authenticity of communications related to financial matters to avoid phishing and other scams. Use official contact details for verification.

List Of Some Popular Online Finance And Transaction App

PayPal offers a secure platform for sending and receiving money, making online purchases, and managing finances. To ensure a healthy and safe transaction on PayPal:

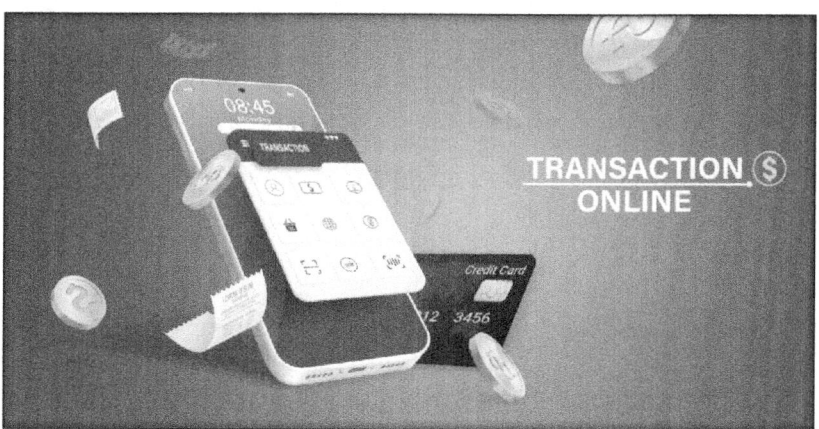

Securing PayPal and Venmo Transactions

PayPal:

1. Use a Unique Password: Ensure your PayPal account has a strong, unique password. Avoid using this password for other accounts.

2. Enable Two-Factor Authentication: Add an extra layer of security by enabling two-factor authentication.

3. Verify Recipient Information: Confirm the identity of recipients before transferring money. Double-check email addresses or phone numbers.

4. Review Transactions: Regularly monitor transaction details. Report any unauthorized or suspicious activity to PayPal immediately.

5. Leverage Protection Policies: Make use of PayPal's buyer and seller protection policies to safeguard against fraud and disputes.

Venmo:

1. Set Up a Unique PIN: Enhance account security with a unique PIN.

2. Enable Multi-Factor Authentication: Activate this feature for additional account protection.

3. Transact with Known Contacts: Only send or receive money from people you know and trust.

4. Regularly Review Transactions: Keep an eye on your transaction history. Report any unfamiliar or suspicious transactions to Venmo's support team.

5. Adjust Privacy Settings: Use Venmo's privacy controls to manage who can view your transactions, reducing potential privacy risks.

Secure Transactions on Popular Digital Payment Platforms

1. Cash App:

- Set a unique, strong password and use biometric security features.

- Transact only with known contacts or reputable businesses.

- Stay alert to fraud and phishing attempts and report any suspicious activity.

2. Zelle:

- Securely link your bank account and use strong authentication methods.

- Verify recipient details before sending money.

- Maintain confidentiality of personal and financial information.

3. Google Pay, Apple Pay, Samsung Pay:

- Use device passcodes and biometric authentication.

- Make transactions with trusted merchants and on secure connections.

- Regularly monitor transaction history and report any unusual activity.

4. Square Cash (Cash App):

- Implement a strong password and security features like Touch **ID or Face ID.**

- Conduct transactions with verified contacts or businesses.

- Be vigilant about fraud and promptly report any unauthorized activities.

5. Alipay:

- Ensure your account is secured with a unique password and facial recognition.

- Engage only with trusted merchants.

- Protect your login credentials and monitor transaction history.

6. Revolut:

- Use a strong, unique password and biometric authentication for your account.

- Transact with reputable merchants using secure, encrypted connections.

- Absolutely, your approach to using Revolut, or indeed any digital financial platform, is spot-on. Being cautious of potential scams and phishing attempts is crucial. Here's a brief recap of best practices:

Safe Usage of Digital Financial Platforms like Revolut

Beware of Scams and Phishing: Always be vigilant for fraudulent activities. Scammers often disguise themselves as legitimate entities to steal your information. Never respond to unsolicited requests for sensitive information or login credentials.

Monitor Account Activity: Keep a regular check on your account for any transactions or activities that seem out of the ordinary. This includes transactions you don't recognize or changes in account settings that you didn't make.

Prompt Reporting: In case of any suspicious activity or unauthorized transactions, immediately contact Revolut's customer support. Quick reporting can prevent further unauthorized actions and potentially help in recovering any lost funds.

Backing Up Data And Mitigating The Risk Of Data Loss

85

1. Financial Loss: The risk of significant financial repercussions due to data loss is profound, impacting both businesses and individuals. It's essential to understand that beyond direct financial loss, indirect costs such as legal fees, investigation costs, and loss of customer trust can exacerbate the financial impact.

2. Identity Theft: Data loss leading to identity theft can have devastating effects, extending beyond financial harm to psychological and social repercussions. Identity theft not only affects an individual's financial health but can also lead to long-term damage to their reputation and personal relationships.

3. Reputational Damage: For businesses and individuals alike, the reputational damage caused by data loss can be long-lasting. The loss of customer trust and confidence can lead to a decline in business and can be harder to repair than the direct financial losses.

4. Encrypted Cloud Backup: Utilizing encrypted cloud backup offers a secure way to store and manage data. It's crucial to choose reputable cloud service providers who comply with stringent security standards to ensure data safety.

5. Local Encrypted Storage: Using local encrypted storage devices like external hard drives or USB drives provides an added layer of security. These devices should be kept in a secure location and used as part of a broader data backup strategy.

6. Diversifying Backup Locations: Storing backup copies in multiple locations helps mitigate the risk of catastrophic data loss due to localized disasters or targeted cyberattacks. This strategy ensures that if one backup fails, others remain accessible.

7. Strategic Planning: Implementing a diversified backup strategy requires careful planning and regular reviews. It's important to consider the types of data being backed up, the frequency of backups, and compliance with relevant data protection regulations.

8. Regular Updates and Testing: Regularly updating backup solutions and testing them to ensure they work as expected is crucial. This proactive approach helps identify potential issues before they become problematic.

CHAPTER 11

Cultivating a Cybersecurity Mindset

Promoting awareness and responsible online behavior

1. **Educating about Cyber Threats:**

   - **Regular Training and Workshops:** Conducting regular training sessions and workshops can keep individuals up to date on the latest cyber threats and defense mechanisms.

   - **Real-life Examples:** Use real-life examples and case studies to illustrate the impact of cyber threats, making the information more relatable and impactful.

2. **Dispelling Myths and Misconceptions:**

   - **Awareness Campaigns:** Create awareness campaigns that specifically target common myths, using simple language and visuals to make the message clear and memorable.

   - **Encouraging Open Conversations:** Create platforms where individuals can discuss cybersecurity issues openly, ask questions, and share experiences, fostering a culture of learning and vigilance.

3. **Promoting Good Cyber Hygiene:**

   - **interactive Tools and Resources:** Provide interactive tools such as password strength testers, software update reminders, and phishing email identification quizzes.

- **Personal Cybersecurity Assessments:** Offer tools for individuals to assess their cybersecurity practices and receive personalized recommendations for improvement.

4. **Exercising Caution Online:**

- **Scenario-Based Learning:** Use simulated environments or scenarios to teach individuals how to react in different situations, such as recognizing a phishing attempt or responding to a ransomware attack.

- **Role of social media:** Conduct sessions specifically focused on the safe use of social media, addressing issues like oversharing, friend requests from strangers, and the potential impact of information shared online.

This proactive approach helps individuals detect and respond to potential threats before they escalate.

5. **Community Engagement and Collaboration:**

- **Cybersecurity Forums and Groups:** Participation in online forums and local groups dedicated to cybersecurity can foster community engagement. These platforms can be venues for sharing experiences, discussing emerging threats, and brainstorming collective solutions.

- **Regular Security Briefings in Organizations:** Organizations can hold regular security briefings where employees are updated on the latest threats and best practices. These sessions can also be a space for employees to share observations and suggestions.

- **Collaborative Security Exercises:** Conducting collaborative security exercises like simulated phishing tests or hackathons can help in understanding real-world scenarios and how collective efforts can mitigate risks.

6. **Ongoing Education and Engagement:**

- **Continuous Learning Programs:** Implementing continuous learning programs, which could include online courses, webinars, and workshops on cybersecurity, helps individuals stay informed about the evolving landscape.

- **Engagement with Cybersecurity News and Publications:** Encouraging regular engagement with reputable cybersecurity news sources, blogs, and publications keeps individuals updated on new threats and innovations in cybersecurity.

- **Use of Interactive and Gamified Learning Tools:** Incorporating interactive and gamified learning tools can make the process of learning about cybersecurity more engaging and effective. Tools like cyber-attack simulations or interactive quizzes can reinforce learning in an enjoyable manner.

Additional Strategies:

1. **Leveraging Technology for Proactive Defense:**

- Utilize automated tools for monitoring network traffic and identifying anomalies.

- Implement intrusion detection systems and use threat intelligence platforms to get insights into potential threats.

2. **Promoting a Security-first Mindset:**

- Foster a culture where security is everyone's responsibility, not just the IT departments.

- Encourage the reporting of security concerns and create easy channels for reporting these concerns.

3. **Personal Accountability and Cyber Etiquette:**

- Emphasize the importance of personal accountability in maintaining cyber hygiene, such as regular password changes and adherence to security protocols.

- Promote responsible cyber etiquette, including respectful and safe communication practices online.

4. **Regular Security Audits and Assessments:**

- Conduct regular security audits and risk assessments to identify vulnerabilities and address them proactively.

Educating the next generation about cybersecurity through integration into formal education curricula is a forward-thinking strategy. Here are some specific approaches and benefits:

1. Early Exposure: Start introducing basic cybersecurity concepts in early education. Use age-appropriate content to teach primary school students about internet safety, privacy, and digital citizenship.

2. Curriculum Integration: Embed cybersecurity topics across various subjects, not just in computer science. For example, in mathematics, teach the basics of cryptography; in social studies, discuss the societal and ethical implications of cybersecurity.

3. Practical Learning: Incorporate hands-on activities, such as coding projects, cybersecurity competitions, and simulations, to engage students actively and develop problem-solving skills.

4. Critical Thinking and Analysis: Focus on developing critical thinking skills. Encourage students to analyze case studies of cybersecurity incidents, understand the consequences, and brainstorm solutions.

5. Teacher Training: Provide specialized training for teachers so they can confidently deliver cybersecurity content. This could include professional development courses and access to teaching resources.

6. Collaborative Projects: Encourage interdisciplinary projects where students from different subjects come together to solve cybersecurity challenges. This fosters teamwork and an understanding of diverse perspectives.

7. Diversity and Inclusivity: Promote diversity in cybersecurity education. Encourage participation from underrepresented groups to foster diverse perspectives and solutions.

8. Career Guidance: Inform students about career opportunities in cybersecurity. This could involve career talks, internships, and mentorship programs with cybersecurity professionals.

9. Industry Partnerships: Collaborate with the tech industry to provide students with real-world experiences and exposure to the latest technologies and practices.

10. Cyber Ethics: Teach students about the ethical implications of cybersecurity, such as respecting privacy, avoiding cyberbullying, and understanding the consequences of digital actions.

11. Parental Involvement: Engage parents in cybersecurity education. This can be through informational sessions that enable parents to reinforce safe online practices at home.

12. Policy and Advocacy: Advocate for policies that support cybersecurity education and awareness, ensuring it becomes a staple in educational curricula.

13. Open Communication: Encourage an environment where children feel safe to share their online experiences. Regular discussions about what they do online, whom they interact with, and what they enjoy can open doors to more in-depth conversations about online safety.

14. Educational Involvement: Actively participate in their digital education. This could mean learning together about online safety, understanding the apps and platforms they use, and discussing the content they encounter.

15. Setting Boundaries: Establish clear rules about device usage, acceptable online behaviors, and time limits. Boundaries should be age-appropriate and flexible enough to evolve as children grow older and more digitally savvy.

16. Leading by Example: Model responsible online behavior. Children often mimic adult behavior, so demonstrating good digital habits, like respecting others online, not oversharing personal information, and maintaining a balance between digital and non-digital activities, is crucial.

17. Use of Parental Controls: Utilize parental control tools to monitor and limit what children can access online. However, use these as a tool for safety, not as a substitute for open dialogue and education.

18. Teaching Critical Thinking: Help children develop critical thinking skills to discern credible information online. Discuss how to identify misinformation and the importance of verifying sources.

19. Cyberbullying Awareness: Teach children about the signs of cyberbullying and encourage them to speak up if they or someone they know is being cyberbullied. Discuss the importance of kindness and the impact of their words and actions online.

20. Encouraging Positive Digital Footprint: Discuss the long-term implications of what they share online. Teach them about the digital footprint and how it can affect their future.

21.Respect for Privacy: Teach children the value of privacy, both their own and others'. Explain why sharing personal information online can be risky.

22. Emergency Response: Create a plan for what to do if they encounter something uncomfortable or threatening online. Make sure they know they won't be in trouble speaking up.

23. Supporting Their Interests: Engage with and support their interests online, whether it's gaming, coding, or digital art. This not only helps in understanding their digital world but also strengthens the parent-child bond.

24. Educating on Online Scams: Warn them about the dangers of online scams and teach them how to identify potential scams.

Leading by example is the most impactful way parents can influence their children's digital behaviour. Parents set a good example for their children to follow when they act responsibly online. Examples of these behaviours include:

Healthcare Industry:

- **Medical Devices:** Cybersecurity measures for medical devices should ensure the confidentiality and integrity of patient data. Regular security audits and updates are needed to prevent unauthorized access and maintain patient safety.

- **Patient Data:** Protecting patient data requires strict adherence to privacy laws and regulations. Encryption, strong access controls, and employee training on handling sensitive information are essential.

- **Telemedicine**: The rise of telemedicine requires secure communication channels. Implementing encryption, secure login procedures, and ensuring the platforms are compliant with healthcare regulations is crucial.

Critical Infrastructure:

- **Energy Sector:** Protecting the energy sector's control systems from cyberattacks is crucial for national security. This includes robust security protocols, real-time monitoring, and incident response plans to address potential threats swiftly.

- **Transportation:** Cybersecurity in transportation involves securing communication and navigation systems, traffic management systems, and safeguarding against threats that could disrupt transportation services.

- **Public Services:** For public services, cybersecurity measures should focus on protecting data and maintaining the availability of essential services. Regular training, effective risk management, and collaboration with cybersecurity experts can help mitigate risks.

CHAPTER 12

Emerging Technologies and Risks

1. Diversity and Volume of Devices: The vast number of different IoT devices, often with limited processing power and inadequate security features, creates a large attack surface for cybercriminals.

2. New Attack Vectors: IoT's interconnected nature opens up new vulnerabilities, making networks susceptible to various cyberattacks.

3. Weak Authentication and Access Control: Many IoT devices are deployed with default or weak credentials, increasing the risk of unauthorized access.

4.Data Privacy Concerns: IoT devices collect vast amounts of sensitive data, raising significant privacy concerns.

5. Need for Industry-Wide Security Standards: The development of comprehensive standards and best practices is crucial for securing IoT ecosystems.

6. Blockchain and AI as Potential Solutions: Leveraging blockchain for secure, decentralized transactions and AI for threat detection can significantly enhance IoT security.

7. Real-Time Analysis and Anomaly Detection: AI algorithms can analyze data streams from countless IoT devices in real time. They're adept at identifying patterns and, more importantly, spotting deviations from these patterns, indicating potential security breaches or anomalies.

8. Predictive Threat Mitigation: AI systems can predict vulnerabilities and potential attack vectors by learning from historical data. This predictive capability allows for preemptive actions to strengthen security postures before an attack occurs.

9. Automated Responses: In the event of a detected threat, AI systems can initiate automated responses. This includes isolating affected devices, blocking suspicious activities, or implementing corrective protocols, all in real-time and often without the need for human intervention.

10. Adaptive Security Postures: As AI systems learn from ongoing interactions and threats, they adapt and evolve their security strategies. This continuous learning process ensures that defenses are always updated to counter the latest cyber threats.

11. Scalability and Efficiency: AI can manage and secure large-scale IoT environments more efficiently than human-operated systems. This scalability is essential as the number of IoT devices continues to grow exponentially.

12. Enhanced Privacy Protection: AI algorithms can also be designed to protect user privacy, ensuring that sensitive data collected by IoT devices is handled securely, in compliance with privacy laws and regulations.

Predictions For Emerging Cybersecurity Trends And Technologies

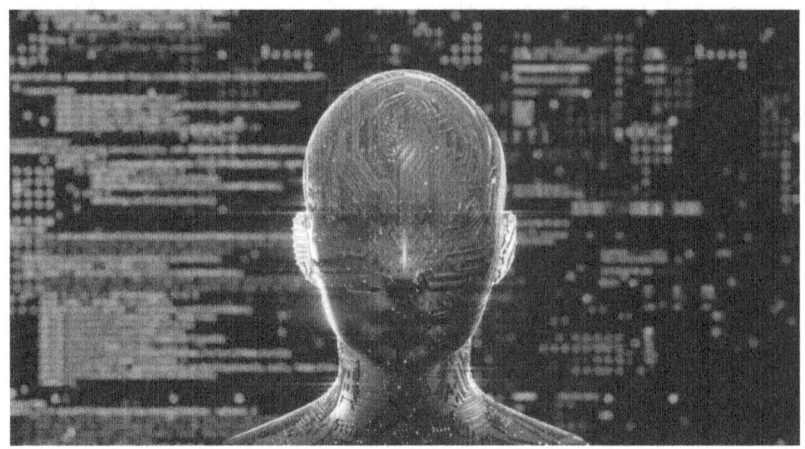

1. AI and Machine Learning: AI and ML are transforming cybersecurity by enhancing real-time threat detection, automated response, and adaptive defenses. These technologies enable organizations to predict and preempt threats, rank security warnings for further investigation, and streamline security operations. The ability to analyze vast collections of threat indicators makes AI-driven systems crucial for recognizing and responding to cyber threats swiftly.

2. Zero Trust Architecture (ZTA): ZTA shifts the focus from perimeter-based security models to a strategy that does not inherently trust any entity inside or outside the network. This approach emphasizes least-privilege access, micro segmentation, and continuous monitoring to minimize potential insider threats and contain security breaches.

3. Quantum Cryptography: As quantum computing advances, quantum cryptography becomes increasingly significant for safeguarding communications against future quantum attacks. Quantum Key Distribution (QKD) is a pioneering mechanism in this space, offering unprecedented security for cryptographic keys.

4. Secure Access Service Edge (SASE): SASE converges networking and security into a cloud-based service, enabling organizations to deliver secure and seamless connectivity to a distributed workforce. SASE combines various security functions with network infrastructure, supporting zero-trust principles and adapting to shifting business needs.

5. Internet of Things (IoT) Security: The surge of IoT devices introduces new vulnerabilities. Effective IoT security involves robust device authentication, data encryption, proactive vulnerability management, and collaborative efforts to standardize security practices across the IoT ecosystem.

6. Privacy-Preserving Technologies: In response to increasing data privacy concerns, technologies like Differential Privacy, Homomorphic Encryption, and Federated Learning are gaining traction. These technologies enable data-driven innovation while respecting individual privacy, highlighting the importance of adopting a Privacy-by-Design approach.

CHAPTER 13

Enhancing CCTV Security Practices

Understanding The Role of CCTV In Cybersecurity

1. Real-Time Monitoring and Surveillance: CCTV systems offer continuous monitoring of critical areas within an organization. This capability is crucial for identifying unauthorized physical access to sensitive spaces, such as server rooms or data centers, where crucial digital assets are housed.

2. Deterrence Against Malicious Activities: The presence of CCTV cameras acts as a significant deterrent to potential intruders or insider threats. Knowing that their actions are being monitored, malicious actors may be less inclined to attempt a breach or any unauthorized access.

3. Advanced Security Features: Modern CCTV systems are equipped with advanced technologies like motion detection, facial recognition, and integration with alarm systems. These features enable quick detection and alerting of unusual activities, providing an additional layer of security and enhancing the overall response capability of cybersecurity teams.

4. Incident Response and Notification: CCTV systems can be configured to send automatic alerts in response to specific triggers, such as unauthorized entry into restricted areas. This immediate notification allows security personnel to respond swiftly to potential security incidents, possibly preventing a breach or mitigating its impact.

5. Forensic Analysis and Investigation: In the aftermath of a cybersecurity incident, CCTV footage becomes a valuable asset for forensic investigation. It helps in piecing together the sequence of events leading up to the incident and can provide visual evidence of the individuals involved. This information is critical in understanding how the breach occurred and in developing strategies to prevent future incidents.

6. Integration with Cybersecurity Protocols: CCTV systems can be integrated with an organization's broader cybersecurity framework, creating a cohesive defense mechanism. This integration might include linking camera feeds with access control systems or network security solutions, providing a comprehensive view of security-related events.

7. Physical and Digital Convergence: The effective use of CCTV in cybersecurity symbolizes the convergence of physical and digital security. This holistic approach is increasingly important as the boundaries between physical and digital worlds blur, with cyberattacks often having real-world implications.

Implementing Best Practices To Safeguard CCTV Systems From Cyber Threats

1. **Robust Authentication Mechanisms:**

   - Limit access to CCTV systems to authorized personnel only.

   - Implement strong passwords and multi-factor authentication to reduce unauthorized access risks.

2. **Regular Software Updates and Patches:**

   - Regularly update CCTV firmware and software to address vulnerabilities.

   - Ensure these updates are applied promptly to protect against emerging threats.

3. **Data Encryption:**

   - Encrypt data transmitted by CCTV cameras to ensure its confidentiality and integrity.

   - Apply encryption to both data in transit and data at rest.

4. **Network Segmentation:**

   - Isolate CCTV systems on separate network segments to limit potential damage from network intrusions.

   - Implement stringent controls on inter-network communications to enhance security.

5. **Routine Security Audits and Vulnerability Assessments:**

   - Regularly assess the security of the CCTV system to identify and rectify potential vulnerabilities.

   - Conduct these audits in line with industry best practices and compliance requirements.

6. **Incident Response Planning:**

   - Develop and maintain incident response plans specifically for potential breaches of CCTV systems.

- Train staff on response protocols to ensure quick and effective action in the event of a cyber attack.

7. **Additional Best Practices:**

- Ensure physical security of CCTV hardware to prevent tampering.

- Use trusted and reputable CCTV brands and products known for their security features.

- Educate and train staff on cybersecurity best practices related to the use and maintenance of CCTV systems.

- Monitor CCTV network traffic for unusual patterns that may indicate a cyber threat.

Exploring Future Trends and Innovations in CCTV Security for Cyber Protection

Integrating advanced technologies into CCTV systems not only enhances security operations but also pushes the boundaries of traditional surveillance. Here's an overview of how these integrations are transforming CCTV systems:

1. **AI and ML Integration:**

   - AI and ML enable CCTV systems to proactively detect threats by analyzing video data in real time.

   - Enhanced accuracy in facial recognition and object detection helps in precise identification and real-time anomaly detection.

2. **IoT Integration:**

   - Connecting CCTV cameras with a network of sensors and actuators creates an adaptable security system.

   - IoT-enabled systems can adjust to environmental changes, enhancing monitoring and response capabilities.

3. **Advancements in 5G Technology:**

   - 5G boosts CCTV capabilities with high-speed, low-latency communication, allowing for advanced edge computing.

- AI and ML algorithms can be deployed at the edge, enhancing real-time decision-making and autonomous operations.

4. **Blockchain for Data Integrity:**

- Integrating blockchain technology secures CCTV footage against tampering and ensures data integrity.

- The decentralized and transparent nature of blockchain adds credibility and trust to surveillance data.

5. **Advances in Edge Computing:**

- Edge computing allows for local data processing, reducing latency and improving response times.

- Autonomous operations in low-connectivity environments ensure continuous surveillance coverage.

6. **Cloud-Based Storage Solutions:**

- Cloud storage offers scalable, accessible, and cost-effective data management solutions.

- Enhanced accessibility and disaster recovery capabilities ensure continuous availability of surveillance data.

Case Studies Real-World Examples of CCTV Systems Defending Against Cyber Attacks

Scenario Overview:

Organization: A global company with extensive operations.

Infrastructure: A vast network of CCTV cameras installed across multiple facilities worldwide.

Challenge: Faced with a sophisticated cyber attack aimed at infiltrating their surveillance system.

Attack Details:

Method: The attackers attempted to exploit vulnerabilities in the CCTV network to gain unauthorized access.

Objective: To compromise the surveillance infrastructure and extract sensitive information from the company's network.

Defense Mechanisms:

1. Advanced Intrusion Detection: The CCTV system was equipped with state-of-the-art intrusion detection capabilities, enabling early identification of the cyber attack.

2. Automated Alerts: The system automatically alerted the security team upon detecting unusual activities, indicating a potential breach.

3. Immediate Response: The rapid response protocol was triggered, ensuring quick containment and investigation of the incident.

Key Strategies Employed:

- Encryption: Data transmitted by the CCTV cameras was encrypted, preventing the attackers from accessing readable data.

- Regular Software Updates: The CCTV system was regularly updated, minimizing vulnerabilities that could be exploited.

- Network Segmentation: The CCTV network was segmented, limiting the potential spread of the attack to isolated sections.

- AI and ML Integration: AI algorithms analyzed patterns and flagged anomalies, contributing to the early detection of the cyber attack.

Outcome:

- **Swift Detection:** The attack was detected promptly before substantial damage could occur.

- **Successful Containment:** The immediate response measures contained the attack, preventing widespread access to the company's network.

No Data Breach: Due to the robust security features of the CCTV system, there was no data breach, and sensitive information remained secure.

Lessons Learned:

- **Importance of Advanced Security:** This case underscores the need for advanced security features in CCTV systems, especially in large organizations with vast networks.

- **Proactive Monitoring:** Continuous monitoring and regular updates are crucial for identifying and responding to cyber threats.

- **Comprehensive Approach:** Employing a combination of technologies like AI, ML, and encryption enhances the overall security of CCTV systems.

Multinational Corporation Case:

Proactive Cybersecurity Approach: Emphasized the importance of regular software updates, robust authentication mechanisms, and data encryption in CCTV systems.

Real-time Alerts: The advanced analytics of the CCTV system provided immediate alerts on unusual network activities, allowing for rapid response.

Incident Analysis: The synergy between CCTV footage and other security data (like network logs) offered a comprehensive understanding of the cyber-attack.

Coordinated Incident Response: Effective execution of the incident response plan, involving various stakeholders, minimized the attack's impact.

Small Business Owner Case:

Strategic Investment in CCTV: Despite budget constraints, the investment in a quality CCTV system with remote monitoring capabilities proved crucial.

POS System Protection: CCTV cameras helped thwart a cyber-attack on the point-of-sale system, protecting customer payment information.

Integration with Other Security Measures: The incident highlighted the importance of combining CCTV with intrusion detection and access control systems.

Maintaining Brand Integrity: The quick action taken based on CCTV footage helped maintain customer trust and business reputation.

Common Themes and Takeaways:

- Adaptability Across Business Sizes: CCTV systems provide scalable and adaptable security solutions suitable for various business sizes and budgets.

- Comprehensive Security Strategy: Integrating CCTV with other cybersecurity measures creates a robust defense mechanism against diverse threats.

- Real-time Monitoring and Response: Immediate alerting and response capabilities are essential in mitigating the impact of cyber threats.

- Post-Incident Analysis and Learning: Analyzing incidents via CCTV footage aids in understanding attack vectors and improving future defenses.

- Investment Justification: The protection offered by CCTV systems against cyber threats justifies the investment, regardless of business size.

Training and Awareness Programs for CCTV Operators and Administrators

A. Threat Detection and Prevention

- Enhanced Monitoring Skills: Operators gain proficiency in monitoring CCTV feeds effectively, allowing them to spot unusual activities or potential security threats quickly.

- Understanding Cyber Threats: Training provides insights into various cyber threats, enabling operators to recognize the signs of a potential attack.

- Preventive Action: Armed with this knowledge, operators can take timely actions, such as alerting relevant authorities or initiating preventive protocols, to thwart potential cyber attacks.

B. Rapid Response and Incident Management

- Quick Decision Making: Operators learn to quickly assess security incidents and decide the best course of action.

- Coordinated Response: Training often includes protocols for coordinating with cybersecurity teams, law enforcement, and other relevant stakeholders in case of an incident.

- Reduced Damage: By responding promptly and effectively, operators help minimize the impact and scope of a cyber attack.

C. Mitigation of Insider Threats

- Recognizing Suspicious Behavior: Operators learn to identify behaviors or access patterns that may indicate an insider threat.

- Proactive Surveillance: Regular monitoring and awareness can prevent insider threats from escalating into full-fledged cyber attacks.

- Creating a Secure Environment: A vigilant operator contributes to a culture of security within the organization, discouraging malicious insider activities.

D. Deterrence of Cybercriminal Activity

- Visible Vigilance: The presence of trained personnel operating CCTV systems acts as a deterrent to potential attackers.

- Security Reputation: An organization known for its strong security practices, including proficient CCTV operators, is less likely to be targeted by cybercriminals.

- Confidence Building: Stakeholders, employees, and clients gain confidence in the organization's commitment to security.

Additional Benefits

- Compliance and Best Practices: Training ensures that operators are up-to-date with legal and regulatory compliance related to surveillance and data protection.

- Technology Adaptation: As CCTV technologies evolve, operators need to stay informed about the latest tools and how to use them effectively.

- Community and Industry Safety: On a broader scale, well-trained CCTV operators contribute to the overall safety and security of communities and industries.

CONCLUSION

Understanding Hackers' Motivations and Strategies

- Insight Into Threats: Knowing why and how hackers operate can inform our defense strategies.

- Anticipating Tactics: By understanding common hacking tactics, individuals and organizations can better anticipate and thwart potential attacks.

Recognizing Common Vulnerabilities

- Software Flaws: Frequently, cyber-attacks exploit vulnerabilities in outdated software.

- Human Element: Often, the weakest link in cybersecurity is human error or oversight, such as falling for phishing scams.

- Network Weaknesses: Unsecured Wi-Fi and poorly protected networks are common entry points for hackers.

Implementing Cybersecurity Hygiene

Regular Updates: Keeping software and systems updated is crucial for patching security flaws.

Strong Password Practices: Using complex passwords and changing them regularly can prevent unauthorized access.

- Awareness of Phishing: Educating about the signs of phishing helps in avoiding deceptive tactics.

- Data Backups: Regular backups can minimize the impact of data breaches or ransomware attacks.

Collective Responsibility and Education

- Shared Responsibility: Cybersecurity isn't just an individual concern but a collective one. Everyone plays a part.

- Ongoing Education: Continuous learning about new threats and best practices is vital for maintaining strong security.

- Community Awareness: Sharing knowledge and experiences can help create a more informed and resilient community.

Real-World Consequences of Cyber Attacks

- Economic Impact: Financial losses from cyber-attacks can be devastating for individuals and businesses.

- Reputational Damage: A significant breach can tarnish the reputation of businesses and lead to a loss of trust.

- Personal Consequences: For individuals, the impact can range from financial harm to identity theft.

Proactive Measures for Enhanced Security

- Multi-factor Authentication (MFA): Adds an extra layer of security beyond passwords.

- Network Security: Secure Wi-Fi and the use of VPNs can protect network traffic.

- Security Software: Utilizing reliable anti-virus and anti-malware software provides a strong defense line.

- Incident Response Plan: Having a plan in place ensures a quick and effective response to any security breach.

REFERENCES

1. **Human-Centered Cybersecurity:** Examines shifting the perspective from viewing humans as cybersecurity problems to valuable assets in cyber defense.

2. **Hacker Profiles:** Analyzes USDOJ reports to understand better the connection between hackers and their methods.

3. **Cyber Attack Anatomy:** Dissects the stages and strategies involved in cyber-attacks.

4. **Cyber Risk Analysis:** Discusses the economic and security implications of cyber risks.

5. **Identity Management:** Focuses on enhancing the usability and strength of one-time password authentication.

6. **Password Managers:** Investigates the usability, security, and trust aspects of password managers.

7. **Data Breach Risks:** Explores the risks and anatomy of data breaches in various contexts.

8. **Data Breach Case Studies:** Conducts a multiple case study analysis on surviving data breaches.

9. **GDPR and Data Breaches:** Discusses the General Data Protection Regulation and its implications for data breaches.

10. Defense Against Social Engineering: Examines methods to protect against social engineering attacks.

11. Social Engineering Awareness: Reviews literature on social engineering attack frameworks and awareness.

12.Social Engineering Susceptibility: Proposes a framework to detect employee susceptibility to social engineering.

13.Encryption Concepts: Provides a technical understanding of encryption in the context of cybersecurity and data privacy.

14.Symmetric Encryption: Discusses symmetric encryption in blockchain and cryptocurrencies.

15.Network Security: Evaluates the effectiveness of firewalls and VPNs in securing a network.

16.Cybersecurity, Privacy, and Trust: Explores the intersection of these three critical aspects in digital environments.

17.Cybersecurity in Financial Institutions: Discusses the importance of information sharing in mitigating cyber-attacks for financial institutions.

18.CCTV Systems: Explores the new functionalities, security, and protection aspects of CCTV systems in digital society.

19.CCTV-Aware Routing: Studies the feasibility of CCTV-aware routing and navigation for privacy and safety.

INDEX

D

E

F

R

S

T

V

W

GLOSSARY

Application: A software program designed to perform specific tasks or functions on a computer or mobile device.

Asset: Any valuable resource or item, such as data, hardware, software, or intellectual property, owned or controlled by an organization.

Authentication: the procedure for confirming a user's, device's, or system's identification to ensure access to resources or data is authorized.

Awareness: Understanding potential cybersecurity threats, risks, and best practices among individuals or organizations.

Bait: A lure or deception cybercriminals use to trick individuals or organizations into disclosing sensitive information or taking malicious actions.

Blockchain: a distributed ledger technology that is decentralized and securely records transactions over several machines.

Breach: Unauthorized access to or disclosure of sensitive information, typically resulting in a security incident or data breach.

Bully: A person or entity who uses intimidation, coercion, or harassment to exploit or harm others online.

Clickbait: Headlines and ads are examples of content meant to grab readers' attention and entice them to click on a link, frequently taking them to fraudulent or harmful websites.

Confidential: Information that is private, sensitive, or restricted and should be protected from unauthorized access, disclosure, or modification.

Confidentiality: The principle of protecting sensitive or private information from unauthorized access, disclosure, or exposure.

Credential: A piece of information used to authenticate or verify the identity of a user, such as a username, password, or security token.

Cybercriminal: An individual or group who engages in criminal activities online, including hacking, fraud, identity theft, and malware distribution.

Decipher: To convert encrypted or encoded information into its original form or plaintext.

Disasters: Catastrophic events, such as natural disasters or large-scale cyberattacks, can cause significant damage or disruption to systems, infrastructure, or operations.

Eavesdrop: To secretly listen to or monitor private conversations, communications, or data transmissions without authorization.

Encryption: Converting plaintext or readable data into ciphertext or encrypted form to protect it from illegal access or interception.

Ethical: Conduct or behavior that is morally right, honest, and responsible, especially in the context of cybersecurity practices and decision-making.

Firmware: Software programmed into hardware devices to control their operation and functionality, often stored in read-only memory (ROM).

Hackathon: An event where programmers, developers, and cybersecurity professionals collaborate to solve challenges or create innovative solutions within a limited timeframe.

Harassment: Persistent and unwanted behavior that intimidates, annoys, or distresses individuals online, often involving threats, insults, or offensive content.

Hazard: A potential source of harm, risk, or danger that could lead to cybersecurity incidents, breaches, or disruptions.

Havoc: Widespread chaos, damage, or destruction caused by cybersecurity attacks, breaches, or disasters.

Illegal: Prohibited by law or regulations, including hacking, cybercrime, piracy, or unauthorized access to systems or networks.

Imprisonment: Legal punishment involving confinement or incarceration as a consequence of committing cybercrimes or violating cybersecurity laws.

Installation: Setting up or adding software, applications, or hardware devices on a computer, network, or system.

Install: To set up or add software, applications, or hardware devices on a computer, network, or system.

Intruder: An unauthorized individual or entity who gains access to or attempts to breach the security of a computer, network, or system.

Investigation: Examining, analyzing, and gathering evidence related to cybersecurity incidents, breaches, or violations to identify perpetrators and prevent future occurrences.

Liability: Legal responsibility or accountability for damages, losses, or harm caused by cybersecurity incidents, breaches, or negligence.

Malicious: Intentionally harmful, malicious, or evil, especially in the context of cyber threats, attacks, or activities.

Malware: malicious software, such as viruses, worms, Trojan horses, and ransomware, intended to interfere with, harm, or obtain unauthorized access to computer systems, networks, or data.

Manipulation: The act of influencing or altering data, information, or systems for deceptive, fraudulent, or malicious purposes.

Masquerading: pretending to be someone else to trick people or obtain access to networks, systems, or data without authorization.

Ownership: Legal right, control, or possession of resources, assets, or intellectual property, including data, software, and hardware.

Peer-to-peer: A decentralized network architecture where participants can directly interact and share resources or information without intermediaries or central servers.

Private: Restricted, confidential, or exclusive access to information, resources, or communications that are not publicly available.

Protocol: A set of rules, standards, or procedures governing data exchange, communication, or interactions between devices, systems, or networks.

Ransomware: Malicious software that encrypts or locks computer systems or files, demanding payment from victims in exchange for decryption keys or restoring access.

Scenario: Hypothetical or possible situations, events, or circumstances used for planning, testing, or evaluating cybersecurity strategies, responses, or solutions.

Scammer: A person or entity who engages in fraudulent or deceptive schemes, including phishing, social engineering, or online scams, to trick individuals or organizations for financial gain.

Security: Measures, practices, or protocols designed to protect systems, networks, data, and information from cybersecurity threats, attacks, or unauthorized access.

Skilled: Possessing expertise, knowledge, or proficiency in cybersecurity concepts, techniques, tools, or practices.

Software: Programs, applications, or instructions run on computers, devices, or systems to perform specific tasks, functions, or operations.

Stakeholder: Individuals, groups, or entities with a vested interest or concern in the outcome, success, or impact of cybersecurity initiatives, decisions, or activities.

Staunchest: Strongest or most loyal supporters, advocates, or defenders of cybersecurity principles, policies, or practices.

Surveillance: Monitoring, observing, or tracking activities, communications, or behavior, especially to gather intelligence or maintain security.

Suspicious: Indicating or arousing distrust, doubt, or uncertainty, especially about potential cybersecurity threats, incidents, or activities.

Testers: Individuals or professionals who conduct assessments, evaluations, or tests to identify vulnerabilities, weaknesses, or flaws in software, systems, or networks through penetration testing or vulnerability scanning.

Third-party: An external entity or organization that is not directly involved in a transaction, agreement, or relationship but may have access to or influence over certain aspects of it.

Thumbnail: A small, reduced-size version of an image or document used for quick identification or previewing, often displayed in file browsers or search results.

Transaction: An exchange or transfer of data, goods, services, or assets between parties, typically involving exchanging value or information.

Trick: A deceptive or cunning action or scheme used to manipulate or deceive individuals or systems, often for malicious purposes.

Validate: To confirm or verify the accuracy, authenticity, or legitimacy of something, such as data, information, credentials, or processes.

Verification: The process of confirming or validating the accuracy, authenticity, or legitimacy of something, often through verification checks, tests, or procedures.

Vulnerabilities: Weaknesses, flaws, or gaps in systems, networks, software, or processes that can be exploited by attackers or threats to compromise security or integrity.

Awareness: Understanding potential cybersecurity threats, risks, and best practices among individuals or organizations.

Automation: Using technology, tools, or processes to perform tasks, operations, or workflows with minimal human intervention or manual effort.

Algorithm: A set of guidelines or instructions used in data analysis and computer programming to carry out a particular operation or address an issue.

Legitimacy: The quality or state of being lawful, authentic, or valid, especially in cybersecurity practices, transactions, or activities.

Made in the USA
Monee, IL
07 July 2026

56548180R00085